James Cox

A descriptive inventory of the several exquisite and magnificent

pieces of mechanism and jewellery

comprised in the schedule annexed to an act of Parliament, made in the thirteenth

year of the reign of His Majesty, George the Third

James Cox

A descriptive inventory of the several exquisite and magnificent pieces of mechanism and jewellery
comprised in the schedule annexed to an act of Parliament, made in the thirteenth year of the reign of His Majesty, George the Third

ISBN/EAN: 9783741191442

Manufactured in Europe, USA, Canada, Australia, Japa

Cover: Foto ©ninafisch / pixelio.de

Manufactured and distributed by brebook publishing software (www.brebook.com)

James Cox

A descriptive inventory of the several exquisite and magnificent pieces of mechanism and jewellery

THE

PREFACE.

THOUGH Mr. COX from the moment the Legiflature benevolently permitted him to difpofe of his Mufeum by a Lottery, has been inceffantly defirous to give the public every poffible information, it was wholly out of his power either to deliver fo particular a Scheme, or fo accurate a defcription of the Prizes, as he wifhed, 'till the intended additions to his fuperb collection, were nearly finifh'd.—That period has at length arriv'd, and he is encourag'd by many of the moft diftinguifh'd names in the fcientific, as well as in the great world, to hope, that the bare admiffion to a fight of his labours, abftracted from the eventual intereft which every Ticket is allow'd in the property, will be univerfally acknowledg'd to deferve even twice the money which procures both that admiffion and that intereft to the feveral adventurers.—In reality, the merit of the Artifts employed on the feveral works which are now to be fold through the medium of his Lottery, is fo very extraordinary, that he can find no words in the whole extent of the englifh language to do them fufficient juftice ; the Reader therefore muft not be furpriz'd if in the courfe of the following inventory, the defcriptions are every moment mingled with epithets of admiration.—

Let

Let him, at leaft, fee the works in queftion, before he cenfures the warmth with which they are defcrib'd, and he will foon find in the greatnefs of his own aftonifhment, an ample apology for the fervour of the defcriber.

It is univerfally acknowledg'd, that in all polifh'd countries the cultivation of the fine Arts has been conftantly attended to as a circumftance effentially requifite, to elevate the character of the people.—Greece is more celebrated for its genius, than Rome is for its dominion; and it is the peculiar glory of Great Britain, that the protection in this age, fo liberally extended to artifts of every denomination, is look'd upon no lefs as an honour to our national good fenfe, than as an elegant avenue to our national property.—The arts, Mr. Cox begs leave to obferve, have their importance as well as their beauty; and we are fortunately bleffed with a fovereign who is perfectly acquainted with their worth ; — they open the powers of the human invention, and furnifh employment for thoufands, — they keep immenfe fums at home, which the opulent would otherwife fend abroad for works of fplendour or ingenuity; and they even bring in immenfe fums from other kingdoms.—Mr. Cox for his own part, is happy enough to have prov'd before the honourable Houfe of Commons, while the Bill for his Lottery was in agitation, that befides giving bread to many large families, his exports have brought more than half a million fterling to the port of London within the laft feven years.—Mr. Cox muft therefore, again remark, that the fine arts are treated much too lightly, when they are confider'd only as fo many minifters of pleafure to a fplendid curiofity.—They are to be weighed in the fcale of utility, as well as in the ballance of ornament, when they either fave or bring us money, and of courfe deferve every encouragement which is given to our moft capital manufactures. —To philofophize and rail againft the arts, as luxuries, is to lay a general axe to the root of all Art and all Science.—The luxuries of the rich, are the chief fources of employment for the poor, and the revenues of the State are collected in a great mea· fure from the luxuries of the whole community; let us not look at luxury then partially, and dwell entirely upon its cafual inconveniencies, when in fact it is the grand ftimulus which gives univerfal being to induftry, and forms not only our chief happinefs as individuals, but our chief greatnefs as a people.—'Tis the

defire of poffeffing the comforts, nay the elegancies of life,
that quickens all our purfuits, and without this defire, our national coffers would not only he fpeedily exhaufted, but nine tenths,
of our inhabitants immediately without bread. — If Philofophy
would reduce us to a ftate of paftoral fimplicity, and confine
us to thofe articles which are folely neceffary for our exiftence,
let Philofophy recollect the wretched fituation of feeblenefs,
ignorance, and barbarity, in which thofe countries are plunged,
that have hitherto continued unacquainted with luxury.—The
Aborigenes of America, the Negroes on the Gold Coaft, the
Tribes of Arabia, are all ftrangers to luxury in our fenfe of the
term, and fit down philofophically contented with food, reft,
and covering.—Yet who will venture to fay that the contracted
circle of their wants, has made them happier, wifer, or more
formidable than thofe nations in which luxury has moft exten-
fively fown the numberlefs demands of artificial neceffity.—
Little as they have to contend for, they are engaged in almoft
perpetual hoftilities; and few as their wants are, they find a
greater difficulty in fatisfying them, than we do in the acqui-
fition of our principal enjoyments —Their utter unacquaintance
befides with that bugbear of philofophy, luxury, neither renders
them more numerous, nor more virtuous, than the fons of ci-
vilization.—On the contrary, they are remarkably addicted to
our worft vices, and fo impotent an enemy, that a fingle Euro-
pean regiment would exterminate a whole nation,—what then
have thefe poor people benefitted by their ignorance of luxury?
This ifland, when its manners were equally fimple, when the
bare earth ferv'd our anceftors for a bed; when the fkin of a
beaft was an appendage of Gentility, and a fine Lady conceiv'd
herfelf elegantly dreft if fhe could decorate her fhoulders with
a piece of an old blanket, this ifland was equally wretched,
barbarous, and defencelefs; nor was it 'till Trade had fo extended the arms of luxury, as to introduce ten thoufand artificial wants, which furnifhed ten thoufand fources of em
ployment for the people, that we were able to make. a figure
among the nations, and formidable enough to repel the invafion
of our enemies. — As Luxury encreas'd, the fine arts gradually
made their appearance, the Sciences were cultivated, and every
man defirous of obtaining the elegancies of life for himfelf,

laboured

laboured to ftrike out a certain method of precuring them.—
Hence originated the noble fpirit of induftry.—hence the powers
of 'the human mind were happily call'd forth, and hence what
Philofophy abfurdly reprobated as the bane, became in reality
the greateft bleffing of fociety.—Superficial reafoners however
are eternally recurring to the *ufefulnefs* of things, and condemn-
ing every art difcriminately, for which they do not perceive an
immediate *neceffity.*—But furely in a commercial country, where
luxury muft conftitute the very foul of Trade, nothing can be
more impolitic.—It has, for inftance, been repeatedly obferv'd
of Mr. Cox's labours, that though they are wonders of ingenuity and fplendour, they were neverthelefs of no real *ufe,*—
but furely they were of great utility, if they brought half a
million into the kingdom.—If for years they furnifhed employment to hundreds, and tended in that employment to en-
creafe the public revenue.—Cafuifts of the nature alluded to,
may on the fame principle tell us, that we can live very well
without Poets, Painters, Muficians, Architects, Statuaries,
Carvers, Gilders, Engravers, and the whole army of workmen
dependent on the fine arts; nay, they may go farther, and tell
us, that we can do very well without Goldfmiths, Jewellers,
Watchmakers, Mercers, Coachmakers, and an infinite variety of other artificers.— All this is very true, and life may
be fupported as our anceftors experienc'd before the Roman
Invafion, without fhoes or ftockings, without hats or wigs,
without filks or velvets, without cambric or lace, without
linen or woollen, and without fending a fingle fhip for luxury,
either to the Eaft or Weft Indies ; but will thefe confummate
Philofophers tell us, how our people in fuch a cafe are to be
maintain'd; how our Trade is to be kept up on their fyftem
of fimplicity, how our Taxes are to be rais'd, and how we
are to prevent the encroachments of our enemies?—If our
Trade extends in proportion to our luxury, and our opulence
is to refult from our Trade, every new manufacture, let the
fpecies be what *it will*, is a real benefit to the ftate, which
ftrikes out a new mode of honeft employment for the people.
— Mr. Cox has, perhaps, been too minutely explicit on this
occafion ; but as it is extremely fafhionable at prefent to rail
againft luxury, without confidering that it forms the great

foundation

foundation of our private enjoyments, as well as of our public profperity, he judg'd this digreffion neceffary as a general defence for the fine arts, and fhall now turn to the particular bufinefs of his Lottery.

THE

SCHEME of the LOTTERY,

Granted to Mr. *James Cox*, of the City of *London*, Jeweller, UNDER THE AUTHORITY OF AN ACT OF PARLIAMENT, PASSED IN THE THIRTEENTH YEAR OF THE REIGN OF HIS MAJESTY GEORGE III. for the Purpofe of felling his MUSEUM in *Spring Gardens*, is as follows, *viz.*

2 Prizes of the value of £ 5,000	——	£ 10,000
2 Ditto ——	3,000	——	6,000
12 Ditto ——	1,500	——	18,000
18 Ditto ——	750	——	13,500
52 Ditto ——	450	——	23,400
100 Ditto ——	300	——	30,000
212 Ditto ——	150	——	31,800
2 Ditto ——	50	——	100
2 Ditto, firft drawn	100	——	200
2 Ditto, laft drawn	750	——	1,500
120,000 Tickets of admiffion to the Mufeum, at 10s. 6d.			63,000

120,404 amounting in all to	——	£ 197,500

60,000 Tickets mark'd A }			
60,000 Ditto —— B }	120,000, at £ 1. 1s.	126,000
	Balance in favour of the Public -	71,500
		£ 197,500

A 4

The

The Mufeum Lottery will be determined by the State Lottery of the year 1774, unlefs there is a difagreement in the number of Tickets, or unlefs any other unforefeen circumftance fhall prevent fuch a determination ; in that cafe, it fhall be drawn in Guildhall, or fome public place near the Royal Exchange, in the State Lottery Wheels, under the management and direction of Commiffioners who have affifted in drawing one or more of the State Lotteries, and in the fame manner as the State Lotteries are ufually drawn and conducted.

If there fhould be no State Lottery in the year 1774, the Mufeum Lottery fhall be drawn within three months of the time, which has been ufually fet apart for drawing the State Lottery.

Perfons fubfcribing for one hundred tickets and upwards, to fend in their names on or before the firft of November next, to the Mufeum Lottery Office, No. 104. Shoe-Lane, Fleet-Street, where *receipts* will be delivered on the following Conditions.

Firft payment of 20 per cent. to be paid on fubfcribing,
Second payment of 20 per cent. within two months.
Third payment of 20 cent. within three months, } From the time of fub-
Fourth payment of 40 per cent. within four months. } fcribing.
    when *Tickets* will be delivered to the Subfcribers on returning their *Receipts.*

Subfcribers to this Lottery for One Hundred Tickets and upwards, anticipating any payment after the firft, to be allowed intereft at the rate of 5 per Centum per Annum, to be computed from the time the money is paid, to the feveral periods abovementioned.

Subfcribers not making good their payments, fhall forfeit their depofits.

The money received for Tickets is depofited in the hands of Meffrs. Fuller, Halford and Vaughan, Bankers, in Cornhill, to anfwer the fole purpofe for which the Lottery was granted.

In order that the Tickets of the claffes A and B, may be upon a perfect equality, the firft drawn Ticket fhall decide in which clafs the Earings and their fellow prize fhall be ; for inftance, if the number of the firft drawn is 30,000 or *under*, then the Earings with the buft of the Emprefs of Ruffia fhall be in clafs A, and the fellow prize in clafs B ; on the other hand, if the number

ber

ber of the firft drawn Ticket is *above* 30,000, then the buft of
the Emprefs and the brilliant Earings fhall be in clafs B, and
the fellow prize in clafs A ; and previous to the drawing of the
Lottery, an account fhall be publifhed in the daily papers of the
arrangements of the feveral prizes, and if determin'd by the
State Lottery, the order in which every prize fhall ftand relative
thereto.

The prizes in this Lottery fhall be delivered to the feveral fortunate adventurers, or their reprefentatives, in three months
after the drawing of the faid Lottery.

Mr. Cox engages for himfeif, his heirs, executors and adminiftrators, to depofit in the Bank of England, previous to the
delivery of the prizes, Ten Thoufand Pounds, to be paid to the
poffefffor or poffeffors of the brilliant Earings and Buft of the
Emprefs, and their fellow prize, if they, or either of them, think
proper to relinquifh the fame to Mr. Cox, his heirs, executors,
or adminiftrators ; the proprietor or proprietors of thofe prizes to
deliver to Mr. Cox, his heirs, executors or adminiftrators, their
determination in writing, within fourteen days after the drawing of the Lottery, whether they will accept the faid Ten Thoufand Pounds in lieu of the faid prizes, or not.

That the fortunate adventurers may have as fpeedy an account as poffible of their fuccefs, the numbers of the Tickets
drawn againft each prize, will be publifhed in the daily papers
during the drawing of the Lottery ; and one month after the
drawing is over, a regular and correct lift of the fortunate Tickets,
drawn againft each prize, check'd and examin'd by the commiffioners or managers of the faid Lottery, fhall be alfo pub-
lifh'd both in the daily and evening papers.

That the fubfcribers to the Lottery may not be incommoded
when they vifit the Mufeum, in the improved ftate of that
fuperb collection, no money will be taken at the door 'till after
the drawing of the Lottery, nor any perfons be admitted without
the Ticket of admiffion, which is fold with the Lottery Ticket,
though to confult the public convenience as much as poffible,
a Ticket will be then iffued at one guinea and a half, which
will

will entitle two perſons to view the Muſeum, but will give no more than one eventual chance in the property.

Tickets to be had at the Lottery Offices in Town and Country.

I THE above-mentioned J A M E S C O X, *do ſolemnly bind and engage myſelf, my heirs, executors and adminiſtrators, to all and every the purchaſers, holders and bearers of any of the Tickets in the ſaid Lottery, to perform in ſubſtance, manner and form, all the articles herein before-mentioned, and have annexed thereto the inventory and ſchedule as deliver'd to the honourable Houſe of Commons, previous to the paſſing of the Act of Parliament, which ſchedule is annex'd to the ſaid Act. In Witneſs whereof I have hereunto ſet my hand and ſeal this thirteenth day of Auguſt One Thouſand Seven Hundred and Seventy-three.*

Sealed and delivered, (being firſt duly   **JAMES COX.**
      Stampt) in the Preſence of

Thomas Monkland, Fleet-ſtreet.
B. Stephenſon, Ludgate-hill.

N. B. The original Obligation, with the above Scheme and Schedule annex'd, under the hand and ſeal of the ſaid *James Cox,* is depoſited with Meſſrs. *Fuller, Halford* and *Vaughan,* Bankers, in *Cornhill,* who kindly take cuſtody of the ſame, for the benefit of thoſe who may be intereſted therein.

A

DESCRIPTIVE
INVENTORY, &c.

Thofe marked with a ＊ are the new Pieces.

The FIRST and SECOND PIECES.

＊ ＊

Superb HORSE and TENT, accompanied with two magnificent VASES of Flowers, conftituting one prize; for which the fortunate adventurer, if inclined to part with them, may receive Five Thoufand Pounds of Mr. Cox, or his reprefentatives.

The Horfe is of exquifite workmanfhip, fumptuoufly caparifon'd; the houfings on its back are fet as richly as art can execute, not only with jewellery in trophies and other fine defigns in high relief, but border'd with a treble row of jewellery, fring'd and taffel'd with pearls; the bridle is equally rich to correfpon with the furniture. The contraft between the gold on the horfe and the richnefs of the jewellery, in which all the colours of the gems are finely imitated, adds greatly to the beaury, as well as the magnificence of this matchlefs piece of mechanifm. The Bridle is held by a golden figure of an Arabian, whofe apparel is rendered gorgeous with jewellery; in particular his Turban and Robe of gold, which are fet with ftones of various colours, in the Afiatick tafte. The Pedoftal on which this Horfe and Figure ftand, is as capital as

I   what

what it supports; it is surrounded by a baluftrade of gold, and contains an exquifite effort of mufical workmanfhip; on each fide there are elegant defigns and curious motions; the ornaments are grand, bold and mafterly; they ftand before a fplendid Tent of gold, ornamented with an aftonifhing profufion of jewellery. The Tent is lined with Mirrors, by which the Horfe is univerfally reflected, and feen in every part to inconceivable advantage. The whole is fupported by a fuperbly gilt Table, upon the right and left of which, are raifed two Stands, fo elevated as to receive two finely imitated Rhinoceroffes; in the bodies of thefe Rhinoceroffes are mufical Bells, which play different tunes. On their backs is a magnificent Ornament admirably chafed, which contains a moft curious piece of mechanifm, that during the playing of the chimes fets vertical ftars and flowers in motion. At the four corners, above the ftars, are flower-pots and bouquets copied from nature, and fet with pearls and ftones of various colours. Over the flowers, on fpiral fprings of gold, are butterflies hovering. Between the flower pots is a curious Clock, which terminates with a larger vafe of flowers, correfponding with thofe at the four corners. This piece is near eight feet high, and ftands in the middle of two magnificent vafes of flowers, No. 2. and No. 3. forming the richeft fet of imperial ornaments ever made, and well deferving a place in the firft palace of the earth.

The two magnificent Vafes of flowers to accompany the Horfe and Tent, and to ftand on each fide of it, are of an octagon fhape, compofed of the fineft avanturine or gold ftone, and lapis blue and gold, overlaid with rich ornaments of dragons, fatyrs; feftoons of flowers, and other fine defigns, executed in the higheft tafte, and decorated with jewellery of every colour, on every fide. The Pot contains a curious chime of twelve bells, playing twelve tunes; and during the playing of chimes, a double proceffion of men, women, carriages, and animals, in a circular form, is feen, paffing both to the right and left. Upon the top of the Pot, in right angles, are rocks, whereon ftand four Storks curioufly made of filver, turning towards each other in fpirited attitudes; near them are feveral lizards; in the center is a large rock, containing

taining a curious Time-piece ; in the center of the rock is fix'd
a moft fplendid Bunch of Flowers, copied with the utmoft exactnefs from nature, in all its infinite variety of tints and
forms, with different colour'd gems.

The flowers are all in motion, being fixed to fprings of temper'd gold, which gives them vibration as if they were blown
by the wind ; innumerable flies and infects, all of jeweller's
work, hover upon and amongft the flowers ; the piece terminates above the flowers with a large animated Bird ; the
different flowers have their different leaves, made of the fineft
tranfparent green, and amidft the flowers and leaves fplendid
ftars of various magnitudes, are introduced fo artfully, as
to move vertically in contrary directions during the playing
of the chimes, which the flower pots contain. The ftars are
of jeweller's work, adding greatly to the elegance and richnefs,
of thofe very capital ornaments, and have been the labour of
many years. They are placed on Pefteftals, which for richnefs,
elegance and defign, correfpond with the reft, and are nearly
the height of the fuperb Horfe and Tent, which they accompany, compofing the moft capital fet of royal ornaments ever
made. A fet much inferior was the year before laft purchafed
for the Emperor of China, and conveyed from Canton to the
city of Pekin, where they remain with the Chronofcope in the
Imperial palace, as lafting monuments of Britifh ingenuity.

PIECE THE THIRD.

*

A Buft of her Imperial Majefty the Emprefs of Ruffia, with
brilliant ornaments, conftituting one prize, for which the fortunate adventurer, if inclined to fell, may receive Five Thoufand
Pounds from Mr. Cox, or his reprefentatives.

This Buft of her Imperial Majefty Catharine II. the prefent
Emprefs of all the Ruffias, was modell'd for Mr. Cox by that
celebrated Englifh artift Mr. Nollekins, from an original pour-
trait in the poffeffion of his Excellency Mon. Moufchkin Poufch-
kin, the Imperial Ruffian Ambaffador at this court, and is efteem'd
a ftriking likenefs of that great Princefs. The brilliant ornaments
that accompany the buft, are a pair of the richeft Earings that
have for many years been feen in this kingdom, and are by
far

far the moft capital now on fale in Europe ; they weigh 44 ca-
rats 3-16ths, and are fet tranfparently ; the drops alone were
feveral years matching, even at a time when the diamonds of
Golconda poured in upon us more abundantly than they ever
did, or probably ever will again.   They are as incomparably
fellowed, as if cut from one divided ftone ; they are of the firft,
and pureft chriftaline water, of the fineft form, the niceft
proportion, and the moft beautiful luftre ; and when an advan-
tageous occafion offers for the fale of fuch a pair, will entitle
the poffeffor, (if difpofed to part with them) to a price far ex-
ceeding the prefent eftimation of them, tho' they are now efti-
mated at 5000l.

N. B. The two before-mentioned prizes, No. 1. and No. 2.
are determinable in the Mufeum Lottery by one number, the
one in clafs A, the other in clafs B, fo that any perfon poffeffor
of the two tickets A and B, will be entituled to both prizes,
as every poffeffor of a double number will alfo be thro' the whole
lottery.

PIECE the FOURTH.

A very large and rich Elephant, fupporting a magnificent
double Gallery and fumptuous Temple.

The terras or pedeftal on which this finely finifhed animal
ftands, is as fplendid and elegant as fancy could contrive, or as
art could execute.   In the center is a large rock, decorated
with branches of coral ; fmaller rocks project in right angles,
upon which leffer trees of coral are placed, with fhrubs and
other ornaments.   Between each rock is a hollow recefs of a
fine green, running from one rock to the other, and united to
the great rock.   Upon the other parts of the ground, crocodiles,
lizards, ferpents, and various different animals are feen in moft
animated forms ; various fhrubs and plants are alfo interfperfed,
and between the gilt rocks are pannels of gold ftone.

This Elephant is the exact model of one of thofe animals
brought from India fome years ago, and prefented to her prefent
Majefty ; it is richly gilt, and caparifoned with elegant ornaments of jewellery ; the back, forehead and neck are adorn'd
with a profufion of embellifhments.   Upon the faddle, on a
ground finely wrought, a four-branch'd ornament is fix'd, extended at the top to receive a large double Gallery and Temple,

which

which it fupports; the fronts of the four branches are fet with
ftones of various colours, and not only from branch to branch
feftoons of flowers (the largeft and moft capital ever made) are
fufpended, but between the branches there is a very bold and
noble ornament in jewellery.

The Gallery, fupported by the Elephant, is furrounded by a
Gothic railing highly finifhed, form'd into different divifions,
in which finely chas'd mafks are placed in uniform directions,
fupporting feftoons of fruits and other ornaments on every fide;
the body of the gallery is alfo enriched with coque de perles,
fixt in frames richly gilt. The ground of the gallery is a plat-
form, even and regular, upon which there is a triumphal Chariot,
with the figure of a conqueror in martial habiliments, attended
by his generals; this chariot is made to go round the gallery,
the horfes being alfo kept in animated motions. Behind the
figure of the conqueror, are trophies of war, and over them a
curious tranfparent time-piece, the movement and motion of
which are feen through the dial. The wheels of the chariot
are fet with jewellers work, and the horfes, men and time-piece,
are ornamented after the fame manner.

In the middle of the gallery is a large plate of looking-glafs,
of a circular form, fupporting two large Swans of filver, which
do incredible honour to the abilities of the goldfmith and the
chafer; thefe fwans move upon the plane and furface of the
glafs, as if fwimming, both in a regular and meandering direction, though there is no mechanifm whatever within them to
create their motion, of which the fpectator may fatisfy himfelf,
as they may be taken off the glafs at pleafure; two cygnets
follow the mother fwan, fwimming after her conftantly, whether her courfe is even or irregular, and the philofophic as well
as the mechanic principles are united in the caufe, by which
this motion is effected. Upon the verge of the pond of artificial
water, at equal diftances, are four richly chafed and finely
wrought ornaments, which fupport a fecond gallery of a leffer
diameter, yet ftill more rich and elegant than the firft; within
this fecond gallery is a finely polifhed ground, and upon
it, a Chariot drawn by flying dragons, with fwifter motion
than that in the lower gallery. A Turkifh lady fits in the
chariot, and behind her a flave holds a rich canopy over her
head; before her is a golden paroquet, and behind, a Turkifh
officer;

officer; in the center is a time-piece of the same construction, as in the other chariot; the mechanism is also the same, and the wheels are in like manner richly ornamented with jewellery.

In the center of the gallery, round which the chariot is made to run, is a most superb Temple; the architectural part is finely designed, and highly executed; the columns and pilasters, the capitals, cornices, and bases, are extremely rich and beautiful; so are the many ornaments that decorate it in every other part. Within the temple is a most capital piece of mechanism, representing a cascade and fountains of water, some of which appear to descend in torrents, whilst others ascend in different directions, equally to the wonder and delight of every beholder. Upon the top of the temple stands a very capital sphere, fixt in a rich frame, which, during the falling of the cascade revolves on an axis in a very curious manner, giving motion at the same time to a spiral worm placed above it, and set with ruby colour'd stones; this worm forms the termination of the building, which contains besides, a chime of twelve bells, playing various tunes, and has such communication with the cascades and fountains, as to make their motion continue and end together.

The roof of the temple is a mass of jewellers work, being cover'd entirely with fine stones of innumerable colours, and the whole building is, in short, an uniform labour of ingenuity and magnificence. The height of this very capital piece is near eight feet; it has afforded great entertainment to many thousands of the most intelligent spectators, who from the first opening of the Museum have particularly inspected it.

PIECE THE FIFTH.

A musical Chime, with mechanical movements.

*

It is contained within a richly ornamented Pedestal, which stands on feet of jeweller's work; on every side within frames of jewellery, are figures, animals, and other pleasing objects in progressive motion: the pedestal supports an elegant toilet dressing glass, and on the back of the glass is a concave magnifying mirror; the glass turns on a swivel, so that either side may be used at pleasure, and is calculated to adorn the commode of the greatest personage.

PIECE

PIECE THE SIXTH.

*

A ditto, in every refpect the fame.

PIECE THE SEVENTH.

*

A ditto, equally rich and elegant.

PIECE THE EIGHTH.

*

A ditto, ditto, ditto.

PIECE THE NINTH.

Two rich caparifoned Bulls.

With houfings of jeweller's work, border'd, fring'd, taffel'd, and fet with artificial gems ; the Bulls befides are adorn'd with garlands of flowers, leaves and branches (in jewellery) as of old when prepar'd for facrifice ; they fupport an ornament, on which ftand four winged Dragons, bearing an elegant Commode, enriched with many embellifhments, and filled with mufical chimes and mechanical motions ; the chimes play upon twelve bells various tunes, with the moft perfect exactnefs. Upon the Commode is fix'd a Clock of exquifite workmanfhip; the Cafe is finely wrought and executed with great fkill ; the Dial is the richeft and moft fingularly elegant that has ever been made ; it is placed in a center of blazing ftars, all of jeweller's work, which move vertically in contra- ry directions, whenever the chimes are made to play; a- bove the Time-piece, forming the moft curious and fingular inventions of the kind, are two ornaments, which, like the wings of a windmill, move vertically in contrary directions; above thefe ornaments is a pyramid of fpiral ftars, and other decora- tions of jewellery, part of which have vertical, and part fpiral motions, at the fame time that they move together horizon- tally, and produce, from the variety of their movements thus blended together, a moft furprizingly agreeable effect.

Thefe fuperb ornamental pieces are placed on very rich pede ftals, compofed of criftal pillars and criftal rocks, corals, reflect- ing mirrors, chafed ornaments richly gilt, and other highly finifhed embellifhments : their height is eight feet.

B

PIECE the TENTH.

One Bull, in every respect the same.

PIECE the ELEVENTH.

A Camel and Bridge.

The Camel is copied from nature, and esteemed a very correct and close imitation of that Eastern Animal; it is adorn'd with a profusion of ornaments in jewellery, form'd in high relief into emblems of music, and other elegant decorations; the caparison is sumptuous beyond conception, border'd, fring'd and taffel'd with real pearl, of which the very elegant bridles are also compofed. On the back of the animal is fixt a rich pavillion of gold, fet in every part with ftones of various colours, refembling the fineft gems of the Eaft; the Canopy of the Pavillion is covered with them, as is almoft every part of the Pavillion itfelf, in which is the figure of an Eaftern Princefs, that moves from right to left, holding in her hand a guittar, form'd of an artificial ruby, in a moft brilliant focket; the figure is likewife fplendidly dreft. In the front of the Canopy is a curious fmall Time-piece, and the Pavillion terminates with a vertical Star, that appears to extend its points; within the body of the Camel is a mufical Chime of Bells, playing various tunes. The Pedeftal of this curious piece is equally rich, fingular and elegant, with the fubject it fupports; it is in form of a bridge of three arches; on each fide, and in front, fhips failing and other pleafing views are feen: the arches are on each fide fet with artificial gems, and between them are large fcollop fhells of jewellery; the bridge is bounded by rocks of gold, placed on borders of artificial water, whereon Swans and other Water-fowl appear fporting; upon the rocks are lizards of various fizes, alfo ftorks with dogs barking at them, as well as water plants, corals, and other curious embellifhments; on each fide the great center Arch are vertical ftars fet with brilliant cut ftones, which are fet in motion, as are the ftars, &c. by a communication with the mufical Chimes contained within the middle Arch. The top of the bridge is decorated with a gold baluftrade, and the whole is finifhed with a mafterly hand of elegance and execution; it is alfo like the Camel, equally rich on both fides.

PIECE

PIECE the TWELFTH.

*

A camel and bridge, in all refpects the fame as No. 11.

PIECE the THIRTEENTH.

*

A Rhinoceros, ftanding on a rock of gold ftone, fupporting an onyx and gold cabinet.

This is made of copper overlaid with gold; the various foldings, which, like a natural coat of mail, compofe the fkin or hide of this extraordinary beaft, are wonderfully imitated by the artift, who executed this truly capital piece of exquifite workmanfhip. In the body is contained a curious chime of eight bells, playing fix tunes, and ftanding on a large rock of the fineft avanturine of gold ftone : In the corners of the rock are four pots filled with flowers of jeweller's work, copied from nature, and fet with artificial gems of the various colours of the flowers; above the flowers on fpiral fprings of temper'd gold, are infects hovering over the flowers. On the back of the animal is a richly chafed ornament, with vertical ftars in jewellery on each fide, which during the playing of the chimes, by a communication with them, are fet in motion, and have a moft pleafing effect. Upon the part wherein the ftar work is contained at right angles, ftand four fmall Elephants, fupporting a rich Cabinet of the fineft ruby-coloured agate, overlaid with ornaments of gold, finely chas'd in flowers and open work ; the front of the Cabinet, which pulls out, contains effence bottles mounted in gold, with a microfcope and perfpective glafs; alfo burning, magnifying, and looking glaffes, a knife, fciffars, and various other inftruments. On the top of the cabinet is a fmall Elephant, fupporting a time-piece of excellent workmanfhip ; above the time-piece is a moft curious globe or fphere, which, by a fecret communication, is fet in motion, and revolves with the time-piece upon its axis in a moft agreeable manner. Upon the upper corners of the cabinet are fixed vafes of flowers in jewellery. This elegant piece is placed upon a ground of crimfon velvet, enclofed within a fhade of glafs, fo as to be preferved from air and duft ; the ftand and frame of the fhade are overlaid and border'd with filver.

PIECE

PIECE THE FOURTEENTH.

*

A Rhinoceros ſtanding on a Rock of gold ſtone, ſupporting an onyx and gold Cabinet, in every reſpect the ſame as
No. 13.

PIECE THE FIFTHTEENTH

*

A Goat.

Made of molten copper, with the cloſeſt exactneſs, and in
every reſpect a highly finiſhed imitation of the Animal: it is
chas'd with great ſkill, ſo that the ſhaggy hair, beard and other
parts are ſurprizingly depicted. —Over the body is an houſing
adorn'd with jewellery, border'd, fring'd and taſſell'd with
pearls; upon the back are richly emboſs'd ornaments in high
relief, which ſupport a moſt elegant caſe of fine workmanſhip.
—At the four bottom corners are Leopards heads, and at the
upper corners golden Eagles with extended wings. On each
ſide, within frames of jewellery, are ſpiral ſtars, the points of
which are all ſet with ſtones; theſe during the playing of muſical chimes fixt in the body of the Animal, are ſet in motion,
and have a moſt pleaſing effect; within the ſpiral points are
center'd vertical ſtars that move alſo by the ſame power. Upon
the top of the caſe which contains the ſtars, at the four corners are flower pots of jewellers work; over the flowers, on
ſpiral ſprings of temper'd gold, butterflies vibrate as if really
alive. A Gothic ornament or railing all of jewellery ſurrounds
the parts where the flower pots are placed, and within the railing are four golden branches uniting at the top, where there
is a large ſun flower finely ſet with ſtones of different colours,
and the whole terminates with a large flower pot, noſegay and
butterfly.

The pedeſtal of this elegant piece is a quadrangular rock,
fixt to the backs of four Turtles; upon each corner of the
rocks over the Turtles, are four figures of Mariner's holding
on their heads baſkets of flowers in jewellery, with moving
butterflies of the ſame. Within the receſſes of the rock both
in the front and at the ſides, are ſtreams of artificial water
upon which Veſſels are ſeen ſailing in contrary directions;
at one end is a Rock of gold, and at the other a Caſtle

through both of which they pass, and make a spectacle incenceiveably attracting.

PIECE the SIXTEENTH.

＊

A Goat, in every respect the same as No. 15.

PIECE the SEVENTEENTH.

＊

A superb Cabinet.

Of the finest and most beautiful red onyx; it is overlaid and mounted in every part with ornaments of gold, richly chafed in festoons of flowers and other fine designs. In the front are folding doors lin'd with mirrors, which when opened discover the draws of the Cabinet; these draws are fronted with chrystal finely cut and overlaid with gold to correspond with the Cabinet; the upper draw contains a great number of fine instruments and essence bottles mounted in gold; the under draw contains the key of a most curious time piece, which when wound up gives motion to a sphere of gold, revolving on its axis during the going of the time-piece. At the corners of the Cabinet are golden vases fill'd with flowers of pearls and jewellers work, above which, on spiral springs of temper'd gold, are insects that move with the smallest touch as if hovering over the flowers; above the sphere is a larger nosegay suitable to those at the corners, and terminating the whole.

In the bottom part of the Cabinet is a most curious chime of bells, playing various tunes; at the four corners are four bulls that support it; they stand on a gilt rock, in the front of which is a cascade and running stream of artificial water, where Swans are seen swimming in contrary directions; at the corners of the rocks are Dragons with extended wings. The Cabinet stands upon a pedestal of crimson velvet, with a glass shade, the frames both of the shade and pedestal are cover'd with silver, by which the whole is kept from air and dust.

PIECE the EIGHTEENTH.

＊

A superb Cabinet, in every respect the same as No. 17.

B 3 　　　　　PIECE

PIECE the NINETEENTH
A muſical Chime with rockwork.

*

In a rich quadrangular ſtand is contained a muſical chime of bells; on each ſide, alſo at each end within frames of jeweller's work, are perſpective repreſentations of a foreſt, with diſtant proſpects; and during the playing of the chimes, Lyons, Tygers, Leopards, Panthers, and a number of other ferocious animals iſſue from the foreſt, paſs along, and at a diſtance horſemen are ſeen likewiſe in motion. Upon this ſuperb pedeſtal ſtands a Rock compos'd of ores, ſpars, foſſils, petrefactions, corals and corallines, and upon the protuberance of the Rock are ſtorks form'd of ſilver finely executed.

PIECE the TWENTIETH.
A muſical Chime with mechanical motions.

*

This is contained within a rich pedeſtal ornamented on every ſide with ſtones of different colours, and within frames of jewellers work, are perſpective repreſentations of men, women, animals, carriages and other pleaſing objects in motion; the feet of the pedeſtal are richly ornamented, and upon the center of it, is placed a toilet dreſſing glaſs in a finely wrought frame, contrived to turn on a ſwivel. At the back of the glaſs is a concave magnifying mirror; the top of the ſtand is contriv'd to take off, ſo that the curious conſtruction, the pleaſing motion, and highly finiſh'd execution of the mechaniſm may be ſeen, and in caſe of accident rectified with facility. This piece is adapted to adorn the Commode or Cabinet of the greateſt perſonage.

PIECE the TWENTY-FIRST.
A rich Vaſe ſupported by Turtles.

*

It is modell'd from the antique, has a large extending foot that reſts upon the backs of four Turtles; it is chas'd and ornamented both in the front and on the ſides, with ſuitable decorations; dragons and other deſigns are fixt to the handles and top of the Vaſe, from which proceed four finely wrought branches, forming a very rich and elegant girandole.

dole. This Vafe is elevated on a rich pedeſtal containing an organ of curious workmanſhip, playing ten tunes.

PIECE the TWENTY-SECOND.

*

A rich vafe ſupported by Turtles, in every reſpeėt the fame as No. 21.

PIECE the TWENTY-THIRD.
A Goat.

*

The Animal is in every reſpeėt the fame as No. 14 and 15; the houſing is alſo of pearls and jewellers work; this goat contains in its body a muſical chime which plays various tunes, and gives motion alſo to a vertical and brilliant Sun placed on each fide, during the playing of the bells; vertical ſtars are likewiſe fixt therein. The ornaments of gold and jewellery are the fame as before deſcribed in No. 15. the pedeſtal indeed is different; the rock is ſupported by four Elephants capariſon'd and ornamented with pearls; at each corner are Tartarian figures with javelins in their hands, ſtriking at dragons fixt on the rocks; within the receſſes in front, is a running ſtream of artificial water; feſtoens of leafage finely chafed and richly gilt, hang down on each fide between the Elephants.—At the back and fides on a beautiful green ground, are fine chafings in bas relief, repreſenting a Stag purſued by huntſmen and dogs in full cry. Two of theſe pieces were purchas'd at a great price in Canton, from whence they were ſent with the prefents annually made to the Court of Pekin from that province. This ſtands within a ſhade of glaſs, upon a ground of crimſen velvet.

PIECE the TWENTY-FOURTH.

*

A Goat, in every reſpeėt the fame as No. 23.

PIECE the TWENTY-FIFTH.

*

A muſical Chime with mechanical motions.

It is of a triangular ſhape, ornamente on every fide with jeweller's work, as are alſo the rich feet on which it ſtands; in the front, back and fides are finely painted proſpeėts in

the

the landfcape ftile, with human figures, animals and other objects paffing in progreffive motion. Within the pedeftal is a moft curious chime of bells, playing various tunes, and the chime is fo contriv'd that the top may be remov'd, by which means the curious workmanfhip of the whole machine can be feen, the principle of the mechanifm examin'd, and every part eafily mended fhould it fuftain any accidental injury.

PIECE the TWENTY-SIXTH.
*

A mufical Chime with mechanical motions, the fame as No. 25.

PIECE the TWENTY-SEVENTH.
*

A mufical Chime with mechanical motions equally rich and elegant as No. 25 and 26.

PIECE the TWENTY-EIGHTH.
*

A ditto, in every refpect the fame as No. 27.

PIECE the TWENTY-NINTH.
*

A large eight-day Clock in a richly ornamented cafe.

It ftands upon four fuperbly chas'd and gilt feet, border'd alfo in feveral parts with wrought frames, mouldings, and other embellifhments. At the angles of the cafe are richly chas'd therms, with ornaments of flowers dropping loofely down.—Upon the corners are gilt vafes, and upon the center of the top is an octagon Temple ftanding on a quadrangular ground; at the corners of which are four gilt pine apples. The dome of the Temple is blue and gold, terminating with a gilt vafe; within the Temple is a moving proceffion of the various characters in Shakefpeare's Jubilee. This elegant cafe contains a very excellent mufical Clock playing eight tunes. The enamel'd dial is fixt within a finely wrought, highly embofs'd, and richly gilt frame fupported by Lions couchant. Above the dial are a wind and water mill, a horfe grazing, and a Mafon working. By the fide of the windmill, is a cart, which is both loaded and unloaded alternately ; and is always mov'd by the movement of the Clock ; the Miller moreover is feen defcending from the mill, and the facks are

con-

convey'd to, and placed regularly in the cart 'till full, when it is again emptied, and this succession of changes is continued perpetually. The watermill is, equally curious and pleasing, the river is seen to flow, the watermill to work, and the water to run down under the wheel; the door of the mill also flies open, and discovers the Miller standing within by the side of the hopper, into which the flour descends, and after so continuing for some time, the door closes again and the motion ceases.

PIECE the THIRTIETH.
A large musical Clock.
*

The case is black and gold; it stands upon richly chas'd gilt feet surrounded with corresponding ornaments. Upon the feet which project from the Clock in right angles, stand four Grenadiers or Centinels finely modell'd and gilt, resting on their firelocks with bayonets fixt. Above the Soldiers, at the angles of the case, are four antique therms, finely chas'd and gilt, also as supporters of the cornish at right angles are gilt figures of the four seasons; behind the figures are pannels of leaves and openwork through which the sound of the chimes proceeds. In the front below the door, are chas'd festoons of flowers superbly gilt; over the door is another gilt ornament; at the sides are doors that open, by which the construction of the clockwork may be seen; these doors are chas'd in high relief, in flowers and open-work; they are gilt like solid gold, and so are the doors at the back.

This Clock is design'd to stand on a pedestal, that it may be seen every way to advantage. The doors behind open to regulate the pendulum and the going; the musical barrel by which twelve tunes are play'd upon the bells, is there also visible, so are the motions of the hammers and other parts of the mechanism. Above the rock is a christal dome enrich'd with gilt frames and other ornaments; within the dome stands a gilt figure which strikes the hours and quarters on a bell fixt in the center of the dome, and on the top (terminating the whole) is a golden figure holding in one hand a sword, and in the other a pair of balances.

PIECE

PIECE the THIRTY-FIRST.

An Elephant and superb silver Temple.

The Elephant is copied from one of the finest models ever seen in this Kingdom, which came from Rome; it is acknowledged by every artist that has examin'd it, to be as perfect an imitation as can be executed, and is made of one entire piece. The mechanism contained in the body of it is so finely constructed as to animate the eyes, trunk, and tail to perform the various motions of life, as if in actual existence; it is also most sumptuously caparison'd, the housings are richly adorn'd with jewellery in flowers and other beautiful imitations. Upon the back of the Elephant is placed a superb Temple of silver, containing a very fine musical clock, in the front of which, besides elegant ornaments of jewellery, are cavalcades, which during the playing of the music are set in motion; they are mov'd also every hour, from the same cause. In the attic story of the Temple stands a golden figure that strikes the hours upon a bell placed therein; the pillars, cornishes, arches, balluftrades, and other architectural ornaments of the Temple are executed with great skill, so are the ornaments of gold and jewellery that farther embellish it: It terminates with a figure sitting on the pinnacle of the building, which holds a bouquet of flowers in jewellery copied from nature. The stand or pedestal that supports this truly elegant master-piece of fine workmanship, is compos'd of pillars of copper richly gilt, and beautifully wrought; in the center is a rich basket filled with various fruits, moulded from the different fruits represented, and placed between the pillars of the pedestal which is rais'd from the ground by several steps, and is one of the very distinguish'd pieces of art that have so much engaged the attention of the public. It is near eight feet high.

PIECE the THIRTY-SECOND.

An Elephant and silver Temple, in every respect the same as No. 31.

PIECE

PIECE the THIRTY-THIRD.

A large ſplendid Bouquet of Flowers in a magnificent Amber Vaſe.

This capital Vaſe is made of the fineſt amber in a moſt maſterly ſtile; the ornaments are rich and elegant beyond deſcription, ſo are the works of the jeweller, the modeller, the goldſmith, the chaſer, the lapidary, and every artiſt employed therein. It contains a large and elegant bouquet of flowers copied from nature: the colours of the flowers are curiouſly imitated in the colours of the ſtones with which they are ſet. Large tulips are ſeen unfolding and cloſing as if actually growing in a garden; butterflies and other inſects, are perch'd amongſt the flowers, and terminate with a large horn'd beetle, all of jeweller's work, ſo animated as to wave its wings, and open and ſhut its horns as in real life; the mechanical powers by which thoſe motions are performed are ſo artfully arranged as to be no where viſible; the leaves of every flower are exactly copied and enamell'd with as beautiful tranſparent green; theſe leaves are decorated with caterpillars and ſnails, beſides a moſt beautiful lizard, all of jewellery; the receſs of the Vaſe is fill'd with mechaniſm and artificial waterworks; the vaſe itſelf ſtands on the backs of four moving Turtles, and is placed on a pedeſtal rais'd on columns of chriſtal, finely adorned with gilt ſhells amongſt lively caſcades, and other exquiſite ornaments of gold, and artificial gems.

PIECE the THIRTY-FOURTH.

A capital Amber Vaſe, in all reſpects the ſame as No. 33.

PIECE the THIRTY-FIFTH.

A Stag ſupporting a triangular Temple.

*

The Stag is large as life, exactly and finely modelled from nature; the horns are moulded from thoſe of the creature itſelf; it ſtands on a ground of copper firſt ſilvered, and then coloured with a moſt beautiful tranſparent green, like the fineſt enamel; the Stag is gilded ſo as to have the appearance of ſolid gold; the horns are of copper richly gilt: the figure is covered with a

mag-

magnificent houſing, ornamented with flowers, leaves, and branches of jewellery, border'd fring'd and taſſell'd with pearls. Upon the back is fixed a rich ſtand, ſupporting a beautiful triangular temple, the firſt of the kind ever made; it is covered with gold and jewellery, and contains a fine time-piece with three dials, which from one movement act as if there were three clocks. Above the dials are men, women, horſes and carriages, paſſing before different landſcapes; at the corners are large winged dragons; above them, jets d'eau; in the center a fine caſcade of artificial water: the part fixt to the back of the animal, is ornamented with lizards, flowers and caterpillars of jewellery and other embelliſhments; the whole is eight feet high, and a pair of theſe magnificent pieces, will fill a moſt diſtinguiſhed place in the Muſeum.

PIECE the THIRTY-SIXTH.

✻

A Stag, in every reſpect the ſame as No. 35.

PIECE the THIRTY-SEVENTH.
A Gardener's Boy, large as life, with Pine-apple.

This figure, which is of the moſt maſterly execution, is of molten copper richly gilt; the coat and other parts of the dreſs are embroidered and ſtudded with jewels, the boy's hat is ornamented with a brilliant feather, and he carries on his head a vaſe of *avanturine*, or gold ſtone, and lapis blue and gold, adorn'd with jewellery. The Vaſe contains a muſical Chime, an irradiating Star, a curious Time-piece, and a Pine-apple of exquiſite workmanſhip; the Pine-apple is of ſilver richly gilt: when the chimes play it burſts open, and diſcovers a neſt of ſix birds; in the center of the neſt ſtands the mother bird, form'd of jewellery; the plumage is ſet with ſtones of various colours, and ſhe is ſo exceedingly animated, as to feed her young alternately, moving round from one to the other with a pearl, which ſhe drops into the mouth of each, and by a very ingenious piece of mechaniſm, the pearl paſſes through the young one, and is conveyed again to the mother bird, who all the time flutters her wings, as if agitated by the ſtrongeſt emotions of maternal anxiety, till the pine-apple cloſes. The ground on which the figure kneels is of copper, colour'd with beautiful green, containing

ing various fruits, roots, leaves, infects, and implements of gardening, differently compofed of gold and jewellery.

This piece is placed under a canopy of crimfon velvet, enrich'd with gold and pearls, terminating with plumes of finely gilt feathers. It is lined with mirrors, by which the figure is reflected, and the motion of the birds feen on every fide; curtains of crimfon velvet and gold are fufpended in feftoons on each fide. The piece is fourteen feet high, and efteemed a miracle of art.

PIECE THE THIRTY-EIGHTH.

A Gardener's Boy and Pine-apple, in all refpects the fame as No. 37.

PIECE THE THIRTY-NINTH.

A Palm Tree.

*

This very fingular and curious Tree is form'd of numberlefs leaves, that cover every part of the body, encreafing in fize and length to the top, gradually expanding and fpreading a luxuriancy of branches, and again declining in magnitude, to terminate in a beautiful fymetry peculiar to that celebrated perennial exotic,—The leaves are all of copper, firft cover'd with filver, and then with a tranfparent verdure like the fineft enamel, through which the very veins and fibres of the leaves may be feen. It is ornamented with dates (its proper fruit) alfo with various infects and flowers in jewellery. It ftands in a tub of great richnefs three feet in diameter; the hoops are of large brilliant cut ftones, the ftaves of brown and gold avanturine. Within the tub is a moft melodious chime of bells that rings changes, expreffes the piano and forte with other graces of mufic, fuperior to any thing of the fize yet attempted. The mechanifm which gives motion to the chimes, at the fame time caufes two fnakes made in gold of various colours, fo jointed as to bend into the moft ferpentine, extended, or contracted forms, not only to iffue from the root of the Tree, but (twining round) to afcend to the top where one enters amongft the branches, and difappears, while the other iffuing from below, in like manner afcends; each doing this in regular fucceffions during the playing of the chimes. Upon the ground or terras furrounding the Tree, which is of copper richly gilt, are various fuitable decorations difpos'd with the greateſt propriety.

This piece is the firſt of the kind ever made, is near fifteen feet in height, and defign'd to fill a diftinguifh'd place in the Muſeum.

PĪECE ᴛʜᴇ FORTIETH.

A Temple of Agate, with triumphal Chariots moving on a rich Gallery, fupported by Palm Trees.

A richly caparifon'd Elephant, ſtanding on a magnificently ornamented terras, whereon fhells, corals, reptiles, and a variety of ornaments are placed. Upon the ground, at right angles, are fixed the fupporters of a rich gallery, in which the chariot of Minerva moves round upon wheels of jewels ; it is fet all over with ſtones of various colours, fo as to make a moſt fplendid appearance. The Chariot is fill'd with muſic and mechanifm, it moves round within the firſt gallery, as does a triumphal chariot within the fecond ; in the center of the chariot is the figure of the goddefs, form'd of folid gold, ſtanding under a pavillion ; the canopy is richly embellifhed to correfpond with the figure : a flying dragon, on a fpring of gold fix'd to the chariot, appears to convey it along. The Chariot that moves round the upper gallery, is that of a conqueror, making a publick entry, attended by his generals ; it is drawn by four horfes, animated with the proper motions of life : the gallery forms a border or baluftrade round a golden rock, upon which a Temple of moſt beautiful agate is placed ; within the recefſes of the rocks, and alfo within the doors of the temple, are fountains of artificial water ; the temple is in every part enrich'd with ornaments of jewellery, and terminates with a fpiral ſtar, that feems to extend its points. The decorations about this very magnificent piece, are almoſt numberlefs and indefcribable. The Elephant under the gallery (whofe eyes, trunk, and tail, feem really in a ſtate of poſitive exiſtence) is a maſterpiece of art ; it is fumptuoufly caparifoned, and the whole piece is near nine feet high.

PIECE the FORTY-FIRST.

A large and moft fuperb Vafe of Flowers.

It is the largeft, the moft capital of the kind, and the richeft ever made; the ornaments are in high relief, and finifh'd with a mafterly exactnefs. It is open on every fide, being fill'd with rock-work, upon which are animals blowing down ftreams of artificial water; fwans form'd of filver fwim round the rock, and at every opening is a frame of jewellery; the fides, feet, handles, and all the other parts are alfo enrich'd with the workmanfhip of the jeweller, the goldfmith, and other artifts. The vafe difplays a fuperb bouquet, containing nearly all the flowers of the garden, copied from nature, with the clofeft exactnefs; the leaves of every flower are alfo given, and the bouquet is fet with upwards of an hundred thoufand ftones of different colours, like the fineft gems, by which every fhade of every flower is expreft, not only with a beauty, but with a truth, beyond conception. There are eight capitally large flowers, two in the center, and three on each fide, which by a fecret communication with the mechanifm contained in the bottom of the vafe, unfold and clofe again like nature; all the reft being fix'd on fprings of temper'd gold vibrate with the fmalleft motion, as if blown by the wind; among the flowers, as if perch'd thereon, are various butterflies of the rareft kinds, reprefented in their infinite diverfity of captivating colours, with a nicety inconceivable; the ftones are cut, and proportion'd to every fhade of the infects, as they are to every flower; a work fo prodigious, that for feveral years it employed a great body of artifts, confequently fupported numerous families. Above the flowers, terminating this magnificent bouquet, are two birds on a fpray; one of the birds is perch'd lower than the other; the under looking up with open mouth, is fed by the upper with pearls, and is fo exceedingly animated as to keep its wings fluttering all the time. The mechanifm, by which the whole is perform'd, is contracted in fo fmall a fpace as the foot of the flower-pot; one fpring and one wind-up part, give motion to this combination of wonders, and the entire piece may be fet off or ftopt at pleafure. At right angles, parallel with the vafe, are tritons

striding

ſtriding ſea-animals, each holding a rich girandole. This match-
leſs work is fixt on a magnificent pedeſtal, ſupported by four
gilt columns, at equal diſtances, and is adorn'd with large ſun
and other flowers of jewellery, held in the mouths of four
reptiles; from the top of the pedeſtal hang down, on every ſide,
feſtoons of flowers in jewellery, ſet with the greateſt ingenuity, and enriching the whole with the moſt happy correſpon-
dence imaginable. Within the center of the pedeſtal is a ſpiral
ornament, enrich'd with leaves and flowers of jewellery; from
the top deſcend numberleſs large gilt bails in regular ſuccef-
ſion, ſo as neither to obſtruct nor touch each other; at the
foot of the ſpiral is a golden crocodile, which at the ap-
proach of every ball, opens its jaws and ſwallows it with
ſeeming avidity. In the center of the ſpiral is a large ſtream
of artificial water. This piece is raiſed on a ſtep of gold, and
is nine feet high.

PIECE the FORTY-SECOND.

A Cage of Singing Birds.

It is placed upon a moſt ſuperb commode of gold ſtone and
lapis lazuli, ſet in frames of ſilver and pannels of gold; ornamented with the greateſt taſte and elegance, with trophies and
finely adapted deſigns; the cage is ſupported at the four angles
by rhinoceroſſes, and in the front by an elephant. The commode contains a very fine ſet of bells, that rings changes, and
plays many curious tunes. The doors in front, when opened,
diſcover a grand caſcade of artificial water falling from rocks:
beſides this, freſh ſtreams are poured down from dolphins, and
blown up by tritons out of their ſhell; while a number of mirrors, placed in the cavities of the rock, reflect the whole, and
render the effect moſt pleaſingly aſtoniſhing. Upon a ſuperb
pedeſtal ſtands a cage of incredible richneſs and beauty, compo-
ſed of gold, ſilver, jewellery and agate; it is deſigned from an
elegant architectural plan wrought in ſilver and gold, with an
execution truly maſterly. Under the doors of the cage, ſeveral
birds are ſeen in motion; on the right appears a neſt of birds
fed by the old one; on the left, birds are ſeen picking fruit and
flowers

flowers. Upon the cage is an eight-day mufical clock, tha chimes, ftrikes and repeats, has two dials, and at the right and left of the cage gives motion to vertical ftars in jewellery. Above the clock is a temple of agate, adorn'd with pillars of filver, and ornaments of gold and jewellery: in front, there is a reprefenta-tion of a houfe, with a mill, bridge, people, and other pleaf-ing objects in motion. Above the temple is an hexagonal pavil-lion, in the center of which is a double vertical ftar, termina-ting with a large ftar in fpiral motion, that appears to ex-tend its points. Within the cage are a bullfinch and a goldfinch, all of jeweller's work, their plumage form'd of ftones of various colours: they flutter their wings, they warble, and move their bills to every note of the different tunes they fing, which are both duets and folos, furprizingly melodious, to the univerfal aftonifhment of the auditors.

PIECE THE FORTY-THIRD.

An Automaton playing on a Flute.

This figure is richly habited, feated under a grand pavillion of gold ftone and lapis lazuli, fupported by filver columns of the corinthian order ; the cornices, mouldings, and pilafters, are of the fame metal, enrich'd with gold ; on the top of this pavillion is a fmall but elegant temple, containing an eight-day mufical clock, terminating with a large extending ftar, in the center of which are numbers of fmaller vertical ftars of jewellery, and a Chinefe proceffion.

The automaton, or figure, plays various tunes on a flute of gold, ornamented with jewels, with the ftricteft mufical truth ; the wind proceeds from its mouth, and it actually graces the performance with its fingers. The pedeftal of this very extraordinary piece, is compofed in the fame ftile of elegance, richnefs and defign as that of the bird cage (to'the defcription of which the reader is referr'd) and difplays, on open-ing the doors, a moft curious water-mill, with rivers, bridges, paffengers, waterfalls, cafcades, and other objects, in various di-rections. Behind the water-works is a mechanical organ of excel-lent workmanfhip, playing a great variety of tunes, different bar-rels being fitted to it for that purpofe.

PIEGE

PIECE THE FORTY-FOURTH.

A Pyramid of Fountains.

*

This is a most capital work of art and elegance. It is in form of a piramid, consisting of fountains and cascades of artificial water, moving in all directions, ascending, descending, and running in an almost countless variety of larger and smaller streams. The base is a large rock, in the caverns of which on every side are falls of water; in the front, ships pass and repass, agitated as in a gale of wind ; at the corners of the rocks, at right angles, are many-headed dragons, above them sea nymphs and tritons seated upon rocks, from which issue fountains of water; the nymphs and tritons hold chains of gold, fixt to the necks of the dragons. From the rock ascends the pyramid of fountains ; with various animals having water issuing out of their mouths, from one to the other on every side ; above them is a group of dolphins blowing up multiplied streams of water, united in one large column, which terminates with spirals of jewellery; on each side the pyramid are two beautiful fountains, that terminate in like manner ; between the sea nymphs; above the rock, is an irradiating sun ; below it, a beautiful peacock of jeweller's work, whose plumage is of stones of radiant colours like nature. The sun is fixt in a frame of the finest ruby colour'd agate, decorated with splendid ornaments of jewellery, forming the closest imitation of the most costly gems and finish'd to perfection.

To encrease the elegance of this very capital piece, a pedestal of christal pillars and rocks is made to receive it ; this pedestal is adorn'd with artificial water and artificial gems on every side ; executed with great taste, and by a beautiful contrast with the other parts, affords a most happy, a most delightful variety of fine works, in which every class of artists employed has endeavoured to excel. In the center is a very finely executed boy, drawing a bow, seated on a sea-horse, which is cast from one of the finest antiques in Europe; it is raised from the ground on steps, and stands within one of the richest and most splendid pavillions of mirrors ever made, by which the whole is surprizingly reflected. Upon each side are rich and highly

finished

finished clocks, fixt upon the backs of eagles : above the mirrors is a dome of copper richly gilt, and ornamented in a masterly manner ; the outside of the dome is overlaid with embellishments of gold, upon a ground of filver ; at the top and center of the dome is a rifing fun, whose rays seem to issue from the center, which has an astonishing effect.

This is the first and most capital piece of artificial waterworks that Mr. Cox ever made ; it is accompanied with musical chimes, and displays several hundred motions, which are made to play or ceafe in an instant.

This piece is fifteen feet high.

PIECE THE FORTY-FIFTH.

A Swan as large as life.

*

It is made of filver, the plumage finely copied, and the whole fo nicely, clofely, and artfully imitated, as at a diftance to deceive the moft accurate obferver. It is reprefented as upon the water, and is fill'd with mechanifm, communicated even to the bill ; it turns its neck in all directions, extending it backwards and forwards, and moving round on each fide to the very tail, as if feathering itfelf ; during the playing of feveral chimes that are heard from beneath, it beats time with its bill to every note of the mufic ; and as the tunes change from fwift to flow, or from flow to fwift, its motion changes with furprizing exactnefs. This Swan is feated upon artificial water, within the moft magnificent ftand ever made, and is reflected by mirrors which produce the appearance of feveral Swans. Under the feat is a rock of chriftal finely conftructed and ornamented ; it is mechanically fet in motion to reprefent the flowing down of water, which is alfo fo reflected by mirrors, as to multiply the appearance of water works in different directions. The rock likewife is embellifhed with a profufion of jewellery and other elegant defigns. Above the mirrors is a coftly dome of great magnitude, on the top of which is a rifing fun that terminates the whole, and makes it near eighteen feet high. The rays and points of the Sun feem to extend from a body of fire in the center, and this piece is fo aftonifhingly executed, that many illuftrious perfon-

ages

ages who have feen it, even in its unfinifh'd ftate, have pro-
nounc'd it rather the creation of abfolute magic, than the
production of human mechanifm.

PIECE the FORTY-SIXTH.

The Chronofcope.

In the year 1769 the fellow to this ftupendous piece, was
fent on board the Triton Indiaman to Canton, and now adorns
the palace of the Emperor of China.

This however far exceeds that, and therefore the term
fellow, may in ftrictnefs be denied, on account of many capital improvements; it ftands within a pavillion of mirrors,
upon a ground of red morocco and gold, rais'd feveral fteps;
the Canopy is alfo of morocco and gold, ornamented with
pearls, border'd, fring'd and taffel'd with gold; elegant curtains of crimfon and gold hang in feftoons from each fide.
The pedeftal of this fuperb piece is compos'd of dragons,
dolphins, ftorks and lizards introduced upon the frame, the
borders, and ground of the table; in the center of the pedeftal
at right angles are four Bulls fumptuoufly caparifon'd and
ornamented with feftoons of flowers in jewellery; parrots
befides in rich fwings of jeweller's work embellifh the border
of the table, which is of the fineft variegated tortoifhell; upon
it is a magnificent gallery fupported by eight Lions. The
ground of the gallery is of gold ftone with a double circle
of blue and gold, whereon ftands a richly decorated Elephant
fill'd with mechanifm extended even to the trunk and tail,
which are in motion. This finely modell'd animal paffes
round the gallery, and caufes two figures of gold in Turkifh
habits fitting on the battlements of a caftle fixed to its back,
to play upon twelve bells, feven different tunes both with
their hands and feet. The Caftle is quadrangular, of folid
gold and jewellery; it is enamell'd with the fineft blue, and
enrich'd with various birds and animals; it contains a moft
curious clock with dials on each fide, which in front are
of tranfparent chriftal difcovering the motions of the clock;
thefe dials are divided into three parts, containing not only a
minute, a fecond, and an hour hand, but a fourth, dividing the
minute into two hundred and forty proportions; the fide of
the clock next the tail, is alfo of chriftal, through which

the

the balance and other parts of the motion may be feen; the hands are of diamonds; the furniture of the Elephant is extremely rich in jewellery, and adorn'd with fringes, taffels, and other ornaments of pearls. The top of the caftle is beautified by a gallery rais'd upon pillars and arches of gold and jewellery; on this gallery there are figures placed, which, by a fecret communication with the clock below, ftrike the hours and quarters upon a bell placed in the middle; from this bell afcends a fpire of jewellery compos'd of twelve ftars of different magnitudes, vertical in their motions: thefe are terminated by a flying dragon ftanding between dolphins, waving its wings, and dropping pearls in conftant fucceffion from its mouth.

In the center of the rich gallery round which the Elephant is made to move, is an obelifk of the moft admirable workmanfhip, fupported by Elephants. The pedeftal which is a fquare, contains the mechanifm that gives life to the whole, and by this, ftars, fpiral worms, irradiations, ferpents, lizards, and an endlefs diverfity of other objects in jewellery are fet in motion, and conftitute an appearance feemingly fupernatural.— At the corners are golden eagles with fcollop'd fhells on their heads; above them ftand large flying dragons with their wings fork'd and ribb'd with jewellery. They difcharge from their mouths large real pearls into the fhells at every motion of their wings, and the pearls by an admirable invention afcend again invifibly into the dragons mouths; as one pearl paffes, thefe gorgeous monfters catch it between their teeth and forked tongues; and when a fucceeding pearl prefents itfelf, they let the firft go, and feize upon the other, moving their wings all the time with the moft animated exactnefs. To the backs of the dragons the column part of the obelifk is fix'd; upon the four fides are fnakes upwards of a foot long, and four lizards proportionably long, all of gold, in various colours; and they are fo curioufly jointed, as to bend into the moft ferpentine forms, to extend, contract, or turn their bodies in almoft any direction. This piece is one of the moft furprizing works that art can poffibly boaft of; the fnakes, as well as the lizards, move on the furface of the obelifh, following each other over the fides and corners, afcending and defcending with the regularity of actual exiftence; they

pafs

pafs through vines with which the obelifk is decorated, and numberlefs infects fet with pearls, diamonds, and other precious ftones, fixed on fprings of gold which keep a conftant motion, at the fame time faften on various parts of the vine; the ftalks, the leaves and fruit are all of jewellery, containing many thoufand ftones fet with great fkill, and fo contriv'd as not to obftruct the ferpents or lizards in their motion, but on the contrary fo calculated as to render it if poffible more agreeable. Above the vines in letters of ruby colour'd ftones, is the infcription, *J. COX, London* 1772. Upon the top of the obelifk over the name, is the figure of an old man finely executed, bending under the weight of a large fphere of furprizing execution; the foot is elegantly fet with ftones of various colours. Upon the zodiac are the twelve figns finely wrought in gold upon a red ground; the figure treads on the neck of a ferpent twining round it, holding the tail in its right hand, and the forked tongue in motion iffues from the reptile's mouth.

The revolution of the fphere is parallel with the horizon, and communicated in an almoft invifible manner through all the motions: the fphere is befides fo artfully contriv'd as to move, in a vertical manner, twelve fplendid ftars round the frame in which it is fixt. On the top of the fphere, is an ornament of jeweller's work, upon which ftands a terreftrial globe, enamell'd, and as perfectly drawn and divided as if ten times the fize: the motion of this globe is alfo parallel to the horizon, and it moves a triangle of large ftars round its own frame, both horizontally and vertically at the fame time; it keeps conftantly moving when the other ftars are mov'd, by a curious connexion with the whole machine, and the machine requires but one winding up to give its almoft innumerable parts an inftant animation. Above the globe to make it terminate agreeably, is a large fpiral worm fet with ftones of a brilliant cut; upon this worm is a fmall golden globe fupporting a golden figure of Fame, with a wreath of laurel in one hand, and in the other a trumpet of gold. The fpiral worm by the moft amazing invention, receives from the fixt power, fuch a circular motion, as to appear feemingly winding up without end; and

not-

notwithstanding its motion is quick, yet such is the farther stretch of invention, that the figure it supports turns very slowly round on every side, and does not as we might reasonably expect, by any means participate of a comparative velocity.

Besides the great weight of gold employ'd in this magnificent piece, there are near one hundred thousand stones in its embellishments, including diamonds, rubies, emeralds and pearls. In short, whether we consider the luxuriancy of fancy display'd in the Chronoscope, the miracles of its mechanism, or the magnificence of its decorations; whether we view it as a labour of genius, or a monument of splendour, it may be justly reckon'd among the wonders of the world, and will be an eternal honour to the artists of this kingdom. — The mechanical parts, tho' delicate beyond conception, are constructed with such excellence, and executed with such strength, that nothing but violence can injure them, or prevent them from performing their various and extraordinary motions to a long duration.

PIECE the FORTY-SEVENTH.

The perpetual Motion.

❋

Is a mechanical and philosophical time-piece, which after great labour, numberless trials, unwearied attention, and immense expence, is at length brought to perfection; from this piece, by an union of the mechanic and philosophic principles, a motion is obtained that will continue for ever; and although the metals of steel and brass, of which it is constructed, must in time decay, (a fate to which even *the great globe itself, yea all that it inherit*, are expofed) still the primary cause of its motion being constant, and the friction upon every part extremely insignificant, it will continue its action for a longer duration, than any mechanical performance has ever been known to do.

This extraordinary piece is something above the height, size, and dimensions of a common eight-day pendulum clock; the case is of mahogany, in the architectural stile, with columns

and

and pilasters, cornices and mouldings, of brass, finely wrought, richly gilt, and improv'd with the most elegantly adapted ornaments. It is glazed on every side, whereby its construction, the mode of its performance, and the masterly execution of the workmanship, may be discovered by the intelligent spectator. The time-piece is affixed to the part, from whence the power is deriv'd; it goes upon diamonds, or (to speak more technically) is *jewelled in every part*, where its friction could be lessened; nor will it require any other assistance than the common regulation, necessary for any other time-keeper, to make it perform with the utmost exactness. Besides the hour and minute, there is a second hand, always in motion; and to prevent the least idea of deception, as well as to keep out the dust, the whole is enclosed within frames of glass, and will be placed in the center of the Museum, for the inspection of every curious observer.

N. B. The very existence of motion in the time piece is originated, continued and perfected from the philosophical principle, by which *alone* it acts.

PIECE ᴛʜᴇ FORTY-EIGHTH.

A superb Sopha.

It is finely carv'd and richly gilt, and besides being embellish'd with a variety of the most capital ornaments, is decorated with convex and other mirrors, in frames of gold, both in front and at the sides. The seats and bolsters are of crimson velvet embroider'd with gold. On the top stands a peacock in all the beauty of the most exquisite plumage, and the eye of every feather is form'd by a small concave mirror, which has a most pleasing effect. Under the peacock is a temple of chrystal, wherein is placed a pine apple in a golden basket. At the sides are pedestals supporting pots of hesperian fruit, with enamell'd leaves. This sofa, if we except its companion, is suppofed to be the richest and most magnificent ever completed; it was intended for the Emperor of China, and by direction made sufficiently deep for two persons to rest thereon a-breadth; it is near fifteen feet high, and artfully contrived to separate into various pieces, so as to be pack'd up and remov'd with great facility.

PIECE the FORTY-NINTH.

A superb Sopha.

In every respect the same as Piece 48. They are both placed at the upper end of the Museum, at the right and left of the throne.

PIECE the FIFTIETH.

The Throne of Gold.

Is thirty-two feet in circumference, of six steps, in a circular form, finely carv'd like a large scoliop shell, and gilt like solid gold ; the steps ascend to two finely adorn'd altars of silver, border'd and embellish'd with gold ; the side pannel is enrich'd with palms and other ornaments of gold, and upon the front, within a wreath of oak, is the cypher of His Majesty in letters of the same metal ; upon the other pannel, within a wreath of myrtle, is the cypher of her Majesty, finely executed. The altars display, in high relief, various attributes and emblems; one is distinguished as the altar of peace, the other as that of concord. Beneath and behind the throne, is a band of mechanical music, compos'd of kettle-drums, trumpets, and other instruments, which perform various fine pieces, and among the rest, the grand chorus of *God save the King*. At the foot of the throne, on each side, are pillars of silver, corresponding in richness, elegance, and design to the altars ; these pillars support two elegant vases, fill'd with flowers of jewellery, copied from nature, and containing not only musical chimes, but mechanical motions, whereby the flowers unfold, and insects move as in actual life. The sides of the pedestal, on which each vase stands, contain various movements and artficial water-works. Above the altars are the pictures of their Majesties, painted by Mr. Zoffanii, on ovals of copper. These royal portraits are magnificent beyond description, being placed in frames of gold, which pour numberless rays, forming sun-beam-like irradiations, in various colours of light, upon the sight of the spectator.

Suspended from above by genii over each picture, are imperial resplendent crowns, embellished with jewellery and pearls, under a canopy of crimson velvet, border'd, fring'd, and tassel'd, not

only

only with gold, but decorated with pearl. Upon the cieling, as well as in the front, imitations of light are apparently descending on the exalted personages pourtrayed. Curtains of the finest crimson velvet, lac'd, and fring'd with gold, fall in festoons from every side, and are join'd at top to the canopy, forming a pavillion, that in magnificence, surpasses even what is related of the celebrated tent of Darius; the pavillion is lined throughout with velvet and gold; around the portrait of the King, is a wreath of golden palm and laurel; and around that of the Queen, another of roses and lillies. The genii which were modell'd for the purpose by *Carlini*, are justly esteem'd a masterly performance, and the whole of No. 50. taken together, is superior to any work, either of art or magnificence, which can be produc'd in any other part of Europe.

Besides the fifty articles already specified and describ'd, as compriz'd in the Schedule annex'd to the Act of Parliament, Mr. Cox, in order to contribute as much as possible to the entertainment and advantage of the public, adds the following capital prizes to the collection, to be drawn against the first and last Ticket of the Lottery.

PIECE the FIFTY-FIRST.
A musical Clock.

*

The case is of the finest variegated tortoishell, form'd into planes, hollows, arches and mouldings; the feet are chased, and of metal richly gilt; the case is border'd round with an ornament in leafage, finely chased and gilt, to correspond with the feet; in the front is an embellishment of grapes and vine leaves, the back is finely decorated, and musical emblems beautify the sides; at the corners, festoons of flowers drop down from rich brackets, supporting the angles of the arches; above them there are other superbly wrought designs, resting on the corners. Over the doors are horns of plenty, and in the middle a crown; the sides and corners are elegantly ornamented

with

with flowers and open work, through which the sound of the music proceeds. Above the arches are burnish'd mouldings, and at the corners vases, chased, gilt and burnish'd; the top of the clock is also of tortoishell, overlaid with embellishments of equal taste and richness as the rest; in the middle is a square pedestal, at the front and back of it, is a bas-relief of an Eastern Prince, fitting under a pavillion of gold; upon the pedestal stands a finely gilt figure, that terminates the whole. This elegant case contains a musical clock, that plays ten tunes, the dial is of ennamel, placed within a border, wrought with great fancy and magnificence; over the dial are perspective views and mechanical motions, equally curious and entertaining. This exquisite clock is placed on a rich pedestal, which contains an organ, the music of which is extremely melodious, and is the first of the kind ever executed; it plays ten tunes.

PIECE the FIFTY-SECOND.
A rich musical Clock.

*

In a case of the finest and most beautifully-variegated tortoishell, standing upon an elegantly embellish'd pedestal, within an organ is contain'd; but it will be needless to enter into a minute description of this article, when the reader is inform'd that it is a copartner in richness, elegance, and workmanship, with No. 51.

PIECE the FIFTY-THIRD.
A curious Bull.

*

With baskets of flowers, moving stars, water works, music and mechanism. The fine model from which this inimitable piece was made, is esteem'd a very correct and close imitation of nature. It is caparison'd and adorn'd with a profusion of rich and elegantly dispofed ornaments in jewellery; it is border'd, fring'd, and tassell'd with true pearls. Upon its back is a basket fill'd with flowers and branches, set with stones of various colours, expressing the various tints of the flowers, in a most beautiful manner, the leaves are actually form'd like nature of the finest green; amongst the flowers and branches, as if hovering

over

over them, are a multitude of infects and butterflies, whose exquifite fhades are as exquifitely preferved in multifarious gems,
by the ingenuity of the jeweller. In the center flower is a curious fmall time-piece, and the bafket in which the flowers are
contained, are embellifh'd with jewellery ; in the middle is an
opening, where a conftellation of ftars, in jewellery, is fo placed,
as to move regularly, with mufical chimes, artfully placed within
the body of the bull, and at the fame time to give motion to a
fall of artificial water. The pedeftal that fupports the bull, is
in form of a golden rock ; at the four corners are four figures
highly finifh'd, finely form'd, and richly gilt, holding pots of
jewellery on their heads ; the flowers are elegantly executed, and
have infects and flies fluttering over them ; the pedeftal is alfo
finely embellifh'd, and contains a curious piece of mechanifm,
that gives motion to fome vertical brilliant ftars, which produces
a moft pleafing effect. The pedeftal is placed on the back of four
turtles, model'd from the life, and the whole ftands upon a
crimfon velvet ground, within fhades of glafs, by which it is pre-
ferv'd from air and duft.

PIECE THE FIFTY-FOURTH.

A curious Bull.

*

With bafkets of flowers, water works, mufic and mechanifm, richly caparifon'd, with ornaments of pearls and jewellery, in every refpect the fame as No. 52.

PIECE THE FIFTY-FIFTH.

A Goat.

*

In the execution of this very capital piece of art, it is ut-
terly impoffible ever to fay enough of the artifts. It is fo
clofe, fo exact a copy of the animal, as to equal any thing of
the kind, ancient or modern ; the fhaggy hair, the beard, the
horns, and every part of the creature are perfectly depicted,
and richly cover'd by the gilder ; the caparifon is incredibly
fplendid, being overlaid and adorn'd on each fide with flowers

and

and ornaments of jewellery, border'd, fring'd, and taffel'd with real pearls. Upon the back, fix'd to the houfing, are four brackets of an emerald colour, extending at right angles, and in the middle is a finely finifh'd figure in an Eaftern habit kneeling, fupporting on its head a bafket fill'd with flowers of jewellery, copied from nature; upon the four green brackets, ftand four fmall, but exquifitely executed elephants, bearing the cabinet of great richnefs; it is made of the moft beautifully vein'd oynx, overlaid with a profufion of ornaments of feftoons, trophies, and other defigns; at the four corners are cherubims with extended wings, looking towards each other; above the cherubims are pots of flowers, the workmanfhip of the jeweller: over the flowers, fixt to fpiral fprings of temper'd gold, are infects in a ftate of vibration; both the flowers and the butterflies are imitated from nature; the various colours and tints of the flowers and infects, are moft admirably expreft in the various colours of the artificial gems. Within the cabinet is a mufical chime of bells, playing various tunes; a rich gilt plate, like mofaic work, of flowers and open-work, covers the top of the cabinet, through which the found of the mufic proceeds. Upon it is a rich pedeftal finely ornamented, in the middle is an elephant grandly caparifoned, carrying a caftle; on the battlements of which is placed the clock or time-piece; above the clock is a rich ornament, fupporting a large vafe fill'd with flowers, correfponding in richnefs and elegance with thofe at the corners; over this ornament, on a fpring of gold, is a flying dragon, holding in its mouth a pearl drop. On each fide the elephant are two pillars, fupporting two Afiatic figures kneeling; each bears a basket fill'd with flowers, and fet with ftones of various colours, in imitation of nature, while flies and other infects vibrate above. This magnificent piece ftands on a pedeftal, correfponding perfectly with it in elegance and fine workmanfhip; at the four corners are four turtles, on which it refts, and on every fide finely chafed in bas-relief, is a reprefentation of a ftag, purfued by hounds and huntfmen in full cry; the animals are richly gilt, on a tranfparent green ground, like the moft beautiful enamel. At the four corners are Tartar figures, arm'd with javelins, pointed at dragons lying on the foot of the pedeftal.

pedeftal. At the upper corners of the pedeftal, are alfo pots of flowers in jewellery; the whole of this piece together, compofing a great difplay of aftonifhing workmanfhip; it is placed upon a crimfon velvet ground, within fhades of glafs, by which it is preferved from air and duft.

PIECE the FIFTY-SIXTH.

*

A rich onyx mufical cabinet, fupported by a large finely eaparifon'd Goat, in every refpect the fame as No. 55.

N. B. As foon as it is poffible to arrange the order of every piece preparatory to the Lottery, the feparate and collective Prizes will be accurately diftinguifhed.

F I N I S.